To: Grandma,

Love is the lesson

the Lord us taught.

Thanks for the Sunday

School lessons.

Happy Birthday!

Love,
Jaclyn

In the Beginning...

The Creation According to Genesis

Henry Holt and Company
New York

1n the beginning
God created
the heaven and the earth.

And the earth was without form, and void;
and darkness was upon the face of the deep.
And the Spirit of God moved upon the face
of the waters.

And God said, *Let there be light*:

And there was light.

And God saw the light, that it was good:
and God divided the light from
the darkness.

And God called the light Day,
and the darkness he called Night.
And the evening and the morning
were the first day.

And God said, *Let there be a firmament in the midst of the waters, and let it divide the waters from the waters.*

And God made the firmament, and divided the waters which were under the firmament from the waters which were above the firmament: and it was so.

And God called the firmament Heaven. And the evening and the morning were the second day.

And God said,

Let the waters under the heaven be gathered together unto one place, and let the dry land appear:

and it was so.

And God called the dry land Earth; and the gathering together of the waters called he Seas: and God saw that it was good.

And God said, *Let the earth bring forth grass, the herb yielding seed, and the fruit tree yielding fruit after his kind, whose seed is in itself, upon the earth:* and it was so.

And the earth brought forth grass, and herb yielding seed after his kind, and the tree yielding fruit, whose seed was in itself, after his kind: and God saw that it was good.

And
the evening
and the morning
were the
third day.

And God said,

Let there be lights in the firmament

of the heaven to divide the day

from the night; and let them be for signs,

and for seasons, and for days, and years:

And let them be for lights in the firmament

of the heaven to give light upon the earth:

and it was so.

And God made two great lights; the greater
light to rule the day,

and the lesser light to rule the night:
he made the stars also.

And God set them in the firmament
of the heaven to give light upon the earth,

And to rule over the day and over the
night, and to divide the light from the
darkness: and God saw that it was good.

And the evening and the morning
were the fourth day.

And God said,
*Let the waters bring forth
abundantly the moving creature
that hath life, and fowl that may fly above the
earth in the open firmament of heaven.*

And God created great whales, and every
living creature that moveth, which the waters
brought forth abundantly, after their kind,
and every winged fowl after his kind: and
God saw that it was good.

And God blessed them, saying,
Be fruitful, and multiply,
and fill the waters in the seas,
and let fowl multiply in the earth.

And the evening and the morning were
the fifth day.

And God said, *Let the earth bring forth the living creature after his kind, cattle, and creeping thing,* and beast of the earth after his kind: and it was so.

And God made the beast of the earth after his kind, and cattle after their kind, and every thing that creepeth upon the earth after his kind: and God saw that it was good.

And God said,

Let us make man
in our image, after our likeness:
and let them have dominion over the fish
of the sea, and over the fowl of the air,
and over the cattle, and over all the earth,
and over every creeping thing that creepeth
upon the earth.

So God
created man
in his own image,
in the image
of God
created he him;
male and female
created he
them.

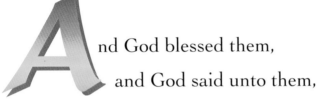

nd God blessed them,
and God said unto them,
Be fruitful, and multiply, and replenish the earth,
and subdue it: and have dominion over the fish of
the sea, and over the fowl of the air and over every
living thing that moveth upon the earth.

And God said, *Behold,*
I have given you every herb
bearing seed, which is upon the face of
all the earth, and every tree, in the which is
the fruit of a tree yielding seed;
to you it shall be for meat.

And to every beast of the earth,
and to every fowl of the air,
and to every thing that creepeth

upon the earth, wherein there is life,

I have given every green herb for meat:

and it was so.

And God saw

every thing

that he had made,

and, behold, it was very good.

And the evening and the morning

were the sixth day.

Thus the heavens and
the earth were finished,
and all the host of them.

And on the seventh day
God ended his work which he
had made;

and he rested on the seventh day
from all his work which he had made.

And God blessed the seventh day,
and sanctified it: because that in it
he had rested from all his work
which God created and made.

These are the generations
of the heavens and of the earth
when they were created,
in the day that the LORD God
made the earth and the heavens,

And every plant of the field
before it was in the earth,
and every herb of the field
before it grew:

for the LORD God had not
caused it to rain upon the earth,
and there was not a man
to till the ground.

But there went up a mist
from the earth, and watered
the whole face of the ground.

And the LORD God formed man of the dust of the ground, and breathed into his nostrils the breath of life; and man became a living soul.

And the LORD God planted a garden eastward in Eden; and there he put the man whom he had formed.

The Paintings

❧ William Blake ❧
The Ancient of Days

William Blake, one of the most iconoclastic and remarkable
of the Romantics, was at once a visionary, a poet, and an
artist. In fact, it is difficult to separate any one of these roles
from the others. Blake's style and imagery cannot easily be
traced to antecedents—he was a true original. He usually
employed his prints and paintings as illustrations (or, more
aptly, "illuminations") of his own writings. Both pictures
and texts were inspired by mystical visions, and though the
images might seem deceptively straightforward, they are
always freighted with countless layers of meaning.

The Ancient of Days, also called *God Creating the Universe,*
is said to have been Blake's own favorite work. In it he
shows God the Father employing architect's dividers to
impose a limit on the world He is creating. Blake's
paintings usually began as prints, which he then finished
by adding pigment. He applied the color to this particular
version of this image when he was on his deathbed.

William Blake, English, 1757–1827
The Ancient of Days, 1827
Relief etching finished in gold, body color, and watercolor,
9 1/8 × 6 1/2 in. (23.4 × 16.8 cm)
The Whitworth Art Gallery, University of Manchester, England
(Details on pages 1 and 2)

❦ Frederic Edwin Church ❦
Niagara

The Hudson River School established that the United States had developed its own art. Earlier, the work of American artists tended to be derivative of European approaches. Here, at last, a group of painters took firm hold of the raw material of American landscape and used their prodigious talents to transform vistas into magnificent works of art.

Church held perhaps the greatest responsibility for this new acceptance. A student and friend of Thomas Cole (see page 57), his work hewed longer and more intently to the style and subjects for which the Hudson River painters were known. Unlike Cole, Church traveled widely and his enormous canvases of sites in South America and the American West are as well known as those of upstate New York.

Upon first exhibition, *Niagara* caused an uproar, becoming the work that many critics—European as well as American—chose as herald of the arrival of an innovative "American" style of painting.

Frederic Edwin Church, American, 1826–1900
Niagara, 1857
Oil on canvas, 42 1/2 × 90 1/2 in. (107.95 × 229.87 cm)
In the Collection of the Corcoran Gallery of Art, Washington, D.C.,
Museum Purchase, Gallery Fund
(Details on pages 6 and 10)

Frederic Edwin Church, American, 1826–1900
Twilight in the Wilderness, 1860
Oil on canvas, 40 × 64 in. (101.6 × 162.6 cm)
The Cleveland Museum of Art
Mr. and Mrs. William H. Marlatt Fund, (65.233)
(Details on pages 8–9 and 36–37)

❧ Frederic Edwin Church ❧
Twilight in the Wilderness

A pervasive current in American thought centers on the conservation of nature in its "unspoiled"—often called its *Edenic*—state. This was a particularly strong impulse in the nineteenth century, as exemplified by the writings of James Fenimore Cooper and, later, Henry David Thoreau. It was also a strongly held conviction of the painters of the Hudson River School. Seldom, however, did any meet the task with such grandeur and near-religious exaltation as Church did in this canvas.

Twilight in the Wilderness is a composite of several sites in the northeastern United States. Church loved hiking and drawing in the vicinity of Bar Harbor, Maine (at that time called Eden), often in the company of his mentor and friend, Thomas Cole (see page 57). Views from that region clearly pertain to this picture. Of greater moment, however, is the idealized vision of pristine natural beauty he presented to his urban audience in pictures like this.

❦ Thomas Cole ❦
Expulsion from the Garden of Eden

When he was seventeen, Thomas Cole's family moved to the United States from England. They first lived in the Midwest, then moved to Pennsylvania and New York State; with each move the painter became more deeply affected by the American landscape. He painted many sites in New York's Catskill and Adirondack mountains and in the Connecticut and Merrimack river valleys of Connecticut and Massachusetts. In untouched nature Cole perceived the hand of God as did such German Romantic painters as Caspar David Friedrich. It is no wonder, then, that he became a founder of what is known as the Hudson River School of painting.

Expulsion from the Garden of Eden was one of Cole's first major landscapes and, along with its pendant, *The Garden of Eden*, it was to point the way toward his more dramatic later canvases, which attempt to capture the transcendental qualities of American landscape and nature.

Thomas Cole, American, 1801–48
Expulsion from the Garden of Eden, 1828
Oil on canvas, 39 × 54 in. (99 × 137.2 cm)
Gift of Mrs. Maxim Karolik for the M. and M. Karolik Collection
of American Paintings, 1815–1865.
Courtesy, Museum of Fine Arts, Boston (47.1188)
(Details on pages 12–13 and 46–47)

Henry Roderick Newman
Wild Flowers

Newman was born in New York, the son of a physician. Destined to become a doctor himself, upon his father's death he persuaded his mother to permit him to study art instead of medicine for one year. His work was well received and he never returned to the medical profession. Poor health caused him to travel to Europe in 1870 and he settled in Florence. His exquisitely rendered watercolors earned him the praise of the English painter and art historian John Ruskin, and he became part of the group known as American Pre-Raphaelites.

Newman preferred watercolor to oil, and *Wild Flowers* shows just how fine his work in the former medium could be. Although well known for his renderings of anemones (the red flowers seen here), it is his observation of the dandelion gone to seed and the surrounding weeds and grasses that is most arresting. They attest to his ability to describe botanical detail without succumbing to pedantry.

Henry Roderick Newman, American, 1833–1918
Wild Flowers, 1887
Watercolor on paper, 15 5/16 × 10 1/2 in. (39 × 26.5 cm)
Gift of Denman W. Ross.
Courtesy, Museum of Fine Arts, Boston (17.1418)
(Detail on page 15)

Albert Bierstadt, American, 1830–1902
Sunset in the Yosemite Valley, 1868
Oil on canvas, 35 3/4 × 52 in (91.7 × 133.3 cm)
Haggin Collection, The Haggin Museum, Stockton, California
(Detail on pages 18–19)

❦ Albert Bierstadt ❦
Sunset in the Yosemite Valley

Unlike other members of the Hudson River School, Albert Bierstadt received his art training by studying in Germany and traveling in Europe. During the first half of his career, his mammoth canvases were eagerly applauded by public and critics alike, but he was working at a time of transition and the tenets he and his colleagues followed were passing out of fashion. (One could argue that late-century industrialization made images of unspoiled nature a bit suspect or, worse, threatening to many collectors and connoisseurs of pictures.) As a result, many of Bierstadt's advocates turned against him.

Sunset in the Yosemite Valley, painted during the first phase of Bierstadt's sojourn in the American West, owes a great deal to the paintings of his friend and inspiration, Frederic Church (see pages 52–55). It aptly demonstrates the younger painter's striking ability to capture time of day and atmospheric effect in the context of majestic nature.

❦ Isaak van Oosten ❦
The Garden of Eden

Animals have been favorite subjects of painters of all ages
and cultures, but it seems fair to grant to Northern Baroque
painters—particularly those from Flanders and Holland—
pride of place for painting them in greatest abundance and
with the most marked naturalism. Pictures of wild beasts or
family pets, gruesome hunting scenes or peaceable kingdoms,
all swell the enormous catalogue of Flemish and Dutch
animal pictures. Often, too, these compositions comprise the
work of more than one artist since painters of the time
specialized in depictions of birds, or hunting dogs, or cattle,
and collaboration resulted in the most expert renderings.

Isaak van Oosten may have been attached to the work-
shop of Velvet Brueghel (see page 68) as he is known almost
exclusively for his exacting copies of that master's works.
The Garden of Eden is a veritable menagerie—cats stalk birds,
penguins consort with swans, and lions stare quietly on as,
in the background, Adam and Eve fall from grace.

Isaak van Oosten, Flemish, 1613–61
The Garden of Eden, ca. 1655–61
Oil on canvas, 22 3/4 × 34 3/4 in. (57.7 × 88.2 cm)
The Toledo Museum of Art, Toledo, Ohio
Purchased with funds from the Libbey Endowment
Gift of Edward Drummond Libbey
(Details on pages 20–21, 23, and 44)

Albert Bierstadt, American, 1830–1902
California Spring, 1875
Oil on canvas, 54 1/4 × 84 1/4 in. (139.1 × 216 cm)
The Fine Arts Museums of San Francisco, Presented to the City and
County of San Francisco by Gordon Blanding (1941.6)
(Details on pages 24 and 40–41)

Albert Bierstadt
California Spring

Bierstadt's *oeuvre* displays some important differences from the works of Church and other members of the Hudson River School (see pages 52–57). Bierstadt was part of a U.S. government survey expedition to the West, so many of his early successes were canvases depicting that vast region, rather than the American Northeast. He also frequently included people, animals, or manmade items in his images, which his colleagues were not as apt to do.

But his masterful ability to capture the evanescent effects of light and weather in order to convey the majesty of landscape is of greatest moment. The huge canvas *California Spring* is a prime example of Bierstadt's mastery of setting and atmosphere. A gentle mist rises over a valley as the naturalistically painted cattle in the foreground blithely graze—all cast with subtle color. His ability to turn observation into an image that captures nature's magic is one of the qualities that make this painter's works of such interest and lasting appeal.

Jean-François Millet, French, 1814–75
Two Bathers, 1848
Oil on canvas, 10 15/16 × 7 7/16 in. (28 × 19 cm)
Musée d'Orsay, Paris (RF 141)
(Detail on page 27)
Photograph: © PHOTO R.M.N.

Jean-François Millet
Two Bathers

When Millet left Normandy to go to Paris to study painting, he became a member of the traditional academic circle of the day. So, some time before works like his *Sower, The Newborn Calf,* and *The Gleaners* shook the French art establishment with their trenchant, perceptive representations of country life, their author was fulfilling his obligations to the academy by painting the requisite nudes and pastoral idylls.

Two Bathers makes it apparent, however, that even when constrained by the strictures of academic painting, Millet was an inspired and innovative artist. This tender image of a couple emerging from the water demonstrates a remarkable, unexpected sense of connection between the two figures, which is at variance with the typical academy-approved approach to such subjects. Considered in this context, the apparent equality of the man and woman is both touching and startling and the couple may be viewed as a modern-day Adam and Eve at ease in their Eden.

🍃 Jan Brueghel the Elder 🍃
Earth, or The Earthly Paradise

The remarkable ability of Jan Brueghel the Elder to render texture and exquisite detail led to his receiving the nickname "Velvet" Brueghel. He was the son of Pieter Bruegel, the Netherlandish painter whose unrivalled works were densely populated with figures, each bearing its own individual, peculiar characteristics.

Jan clearly learned a great deal from his father's work, but he was very much his own artist. In *Earth*, we can see that he developed a style appropriate to his time and place in the Flanders of the Baroque era. Also apparent, especially in the lush color, is the influence of his contemporary and colleague, Pieter Paul Rubens.

This painting on copper was one of four allegories of the elements — Fire, Water, Earth, and Air. It is telling that Brueghel chose to cast the work devoted to Earth as a paradise in which myriad animals — each meticulously and naturalistically rendered — live companionably side by side.

Jan Brueghel the Elder, Flemish, 1568–1625
Earth, or The Earthly Paradise, ca. 1613/18
Oil on copper, 17 15/16 × 26 1/8 in. (46 × 67 cm)
Louvre, Paris (1092)
(Details on pages 28, 30–31, and 33)
Photograph: © PHOTO R.M.N.

🌿 William Blake 🌿
Glad Day

Few of Blake's images combine the literary and mystical
aspects of his talents so magnificently as this. The underly-
ing engraving was made about 1780, but this particular
version was painted fifteen or so years later, in the full flush
of Blake's genius. The color has been added with such
fervor that no vestiges of the fundamental print remain.

Glad Day is as enigmatic as any image Blake ever
created. No fewer than four interpretations have been put
forth persuasively. Some see in it the spirit of England
triumphing over the horrors of the Industrial Revolution;
others suggest that it celebrates Blake's release from
apprenticeship, seeing the youth as a self-portrait. Still
another, more mystical, interpretation makes it representa-
tive of the dawn of what Blake called "fourfold vision"
—the supreme clarity of spiritual insight. But, when
taken as Adam, the figure becomes the universal father-
figure, bursting forth in innocent exuberance.

William Blake, English, 1757–1827
Glad Day, ca. 1794–96
Color-printed line engraving, finished in pen and watercolor,
10 5/8 × 7 3/4 in. (27.2 × 19.9 cm)
British Museum, London (cat. no. 1856-2-9-417)
(Detail on page 43)
Copyright British Museum

Henry Holt and Company, Inc.
Publishers since 1866
115 West 18th Street
New York, New York 10011

Henry Holt® is a registered trademark of
Henry Holt and Company, Inc.

Published in Canada by Fitzhenry & Whiteside Ltd.,
195 Allstate Parkway, Markham, Ontario L3R 4T8.

Library of Congress Catalog Card Number: 95-80843

ISBN 0-8050-4650-X

Henry Holt books are available for special promotions and
premiums. For details contact: Director, Special Markets.

First Henry Holt Edition—1996

Designed by Peter M. Blaiwas

Printed in Singapore
All first editions are printed on acid-free paper. ∞

10 9 8 7 6 5 4 3 2 1